Maegan and Mariah PLAY HIDE AND SEEK

BIANCA HARRIS
Illustrated by Jasmine Mills

To my daughters, I never knew my life's purpose until I created you. You girls are my purest form of joy. I love you both with everything in me, love mommy.

It was a beautiful sunny
day outside. The sun was
shining bright and the
flowers had bloomed.

The girls were asleep, but
Mommy had an idea to
wake them.

Wake-y wake-y sleepy heads.
It's time to start the day.

But the girls were very
reluctant to get out of their
cozy bed.

I have an idea, said Mommy. How about a game of hide and seek to wake you sleepy heads?

Yaaaeee!!!!!!
Shouted Maegan and Mariah.
Let's do it!!!

Mommy started counting.

The girls were running fast, looking for the perfect hiding space.

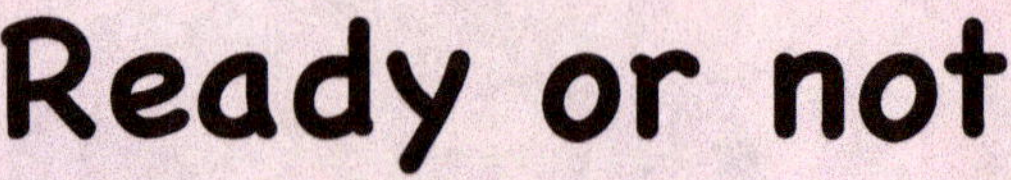

Ready or not

Here I come!!!!!!

Are you girls
under the table?

Are you girls hiding in the bathtub?

Hmmm, Maybe you girls ran outside.

Maybe you're under
the slide,

Or behind the big tree.

Not outside, to my surprise!!!

I must admit, you girls can really hide.

Mommy went back
inside to look for
new places.
But boy oh boy,
look at all the
small spaces.

I got it!!! said Mommy. I know where they are.

Maegan and Mariah are
you back in the room,
maybe under the bed?

I found you!!
I found you!!
I can see you girls' heads.

You girls really love this bed.